First Corinthians 1—7

Have the mind of Christ

by Marilyn Peters Kliewer

Faith and Life
Bible Studies

**Faith and Life Press
Newton, Kansas**

*"For who has known the mind of the Lord
that he may instruct him?"
But we have the mind of Christ.*
(1 Corinthians 2:16, New International Version).

Copyright © 1985 by Faith and Life Press, Newton, Kansas 67114
Printed in the United States of America
Library of Congress Number 85-81041
International Standard Book Number 0-87303-104-0

The publishers gratefully acknowledge the support and encouragement of the Congregational Resources Board of the Conference of Mennonites in Canada in the development of this book.

This publication may not be reproduced, stored in a retrieval system, or transmitted in whole or in part, in any form by any means, electronic, mechanical, photocopying, recording, or otherwise without prior written permission of Faith and Life Press. Unless otherwise noted, Scripture quotations are from the Holy Bible, New International Version © 1973, 1978, International Bible Society.

Design by John Hiebert
Printing by Mennonite Press, Inc.

Have the mind of Christ

Table of contents

Introduction v

SESSION 1. **Quarrels divided their perfect unity**
(1:1-17)............................ 1
Called to be holy in Corinth
Grateful words filled with concern
Cross of Christ emptied of its power

SESSION 2. **Christ the power and wisdom of God**
(1:18-31)........................... 8
The foolishness of what was preached
God chose the foolish things of the world

SESSION 3. **But we have the mind of Christ**
(2:1-16)............................ 16
Resting on the Spirit's power
Expressing spiritual truths in spiritual words

SESSION 4. **God's fellow workers are only servants**
(3:1-23)............................ 24
Dieting on milk instead of solid food
Moving from God's field to God's building
   God makes things grow
   Building on the foundation
   God's Spirit in our temple
   No more boasting

SESSION 5. **An apostle and parent worth imitating**
(4:1-21) 36
Servants of Christ entrusted with secret things
We are fools for Christ but you are so wise
Not to shame but to warn

SESSION 6. **Eat not with an immoral brother**
(5:1-13) 48
Worse than pagan immorality
Be the yeastless bread of sincerity and truth
Expel the wicked man

SESSION 7. **Honor God with your body** (6:1-20) 60
Disputes among the saints
Inheriting the kingdom of God
Bodies for the Lord and not for immorality

SESSION 8. **Marry since there is so much immorality**
(7:1-24) 71
Better to marry than to burn with passion
God has called us to live in peace
   When facing separation and divorce
   Believers caught in mixed marriages
Retain the place in life assigned you

SESSION 9. **Virgins devoted to the Lord in both body and spirit** (7:25-40) 85

Introduction

Welcome to the world of the Corinthians. While the Gospels tell us about the life and teachings of Jesus and the Book of Acts gives us a history of the New Testament times, 1 Corinthians lets us look at a first-century congregation and the problems its members struggled with. This letter puts us in touch with the everyday life of this young Christian church.

During the past few years, as I have been teaching 1 Corinthians, I have found it a most fascinating book. The trials the Corinthian church faced are ones we still struggle with today. As we compare our churches today with this first-century congregation, we may ask, "Has anything really changed over the centuries?"

It seems that the Christian church has always been plagued with divisions, immorality, and questions about marriage and divorce. For this reason, a study of 1 Corinthians is both interesting—in that it deals with many of the same issues as the church faces today; and essential—in that it shows us the way in which Paul the apostle dealt with those problems.

This book is a guide which will lead you into the biblical material. In order to gain most use from this study, follow the steps recommended below.

First, work through the study guide by yourself. Read through the assigned Bible passage several times, watching for particular details, as well as key words or phrases.

In getting acquainted with the passage, consider a number of questions:
* Why did the author write this?
* What did the writer want to share?
* Why is this passage important?
* What meaning do these words have for us today?

If you are working through this book with a group, write down your own answers to the questions before meeting with others. The more each person prepares ahead of time, the more fruitful your discussion will be. Encourage everyone in the group to take part. Be flexible and feel free to use this guide in whatever way benefits you and your group most.

The Bible text used in preparing this study has been the New International Version (NIV).

The New Testament World

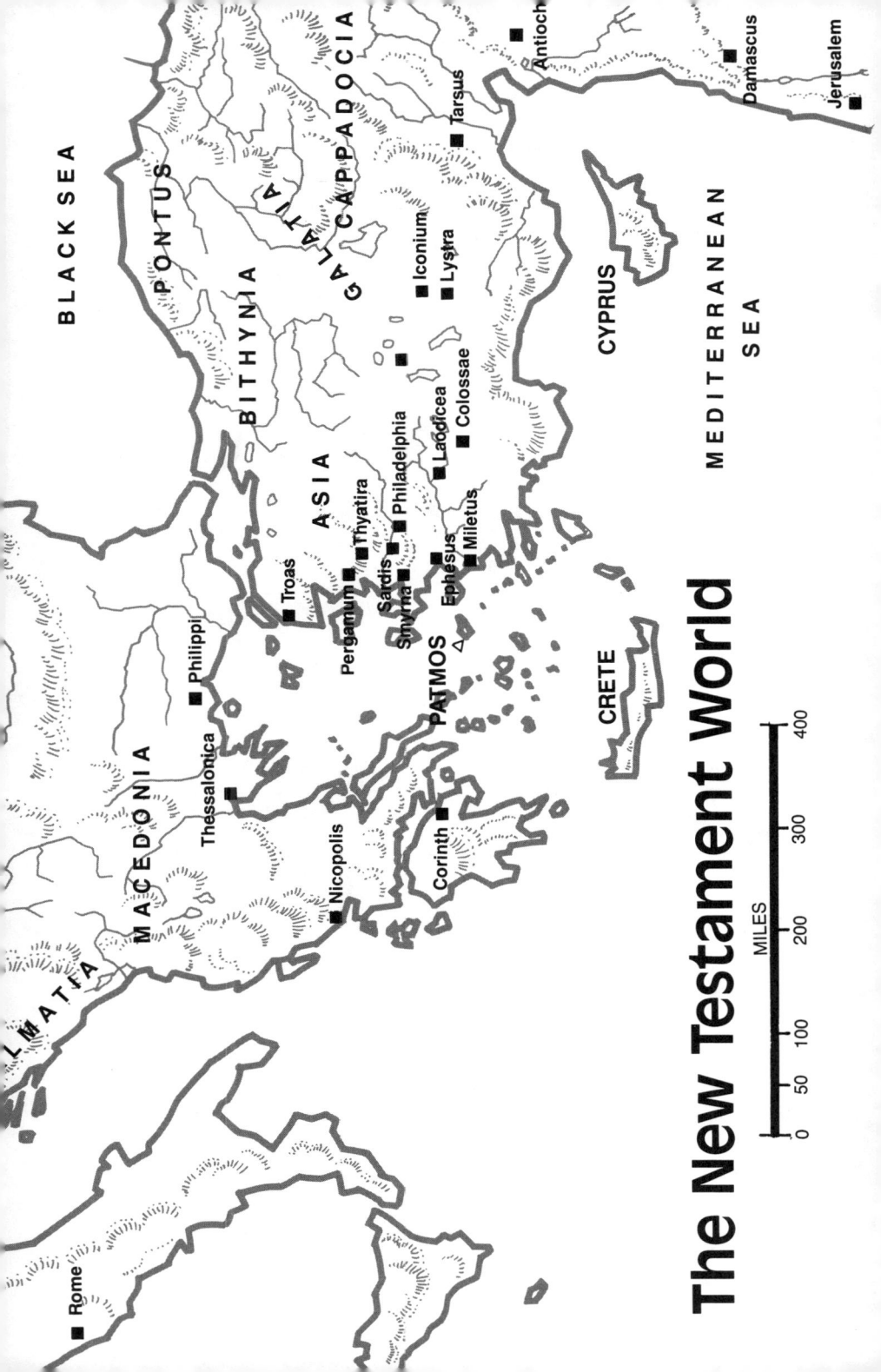

Session 1. Quarrels divided their perfect unity

1 Corinthians 1:1-17

Let's get acquainted with 1 Corinthians. This letter deals with some issues faced by a young Christian congregation. Yet the church in Corinth was a special one with its own location, its own type of people, and its own set of problems in learning what it means to be Christian.

To help us understand the letter, we'll look at who wrote 1 Corinthians and to whom the letter is addressed. In doing so, we'll examine the opening verses, in which Paul, after his opening remarks, quickly gets into a discussion about the divisions in the Corinthian church.

Called to be holy in Corinth: 1:1-3

Any letter follows some kind of pattern. In our letters today, we identify the persons sending and receiving the letter, and we usually begin with a greeting. In the same way, the opening words to the church at Corinth follow a pattern common in the first century. The custom was to give, at the beginning of the letter, the name of the writer, the name of the person receiving the letter, and a greeting. Let's locate these elements in the first three verses.

A. The Writer
   1. Who is the author of this letter? In what special

way does the writer refer to himself here?

_____

_____

Also mentioned in this first verse is "our brother Sosthenes." He may be the same person who appears in Acts 18:17. At the time that 1 Corinthians was written, Sosthenes may have been Paul's secretary, who therefore had a part in writing the letter. The fact that Sosthenes is mentioned here probably means that he was well-known and respected by the church in Corinth.

2. What words does the writer use, in this passage, to show that he has authority and special qualifications? Is this important? Why?

_____

_____

Paul speaks of being "called" (vv. 1, 2). For him, this usually refers to being called by God, and always means being chosen to do a certain task, such as that of being an apostle. For further information on how Paul was called, see Acts 9:1-19.

3. List the things you know about the writer. What kind of person was he? Which of these words do you think best describes his character: brainy? emotional? educated? bossy? humorous? serious? sensitive? To whom would you compare him today? Why?

_____

_____

4. Why is it important to know something about the author? How would a different person with a different personality have written 1 Corinthians?

We have little reason to doubt that Paul was the author of this letter. The style and language of the letter fits with other accepted Pauline writings. He founded the church at Corinth (See Acts 18:1-18.) and kept in touch with the Christians there through letter writing (1 Cor. 5:9; 7:1; 2 Cor. 2:3-4).

First Corinthians was written several years after Paul founded the congregation. He probably wrote sometime during the period A.D. 53-56. The fact that the Christians at Corinth had been Christians for a fairly short period may help to explain why they were faced with the many problems dealt with in this letter.

B. The Persons Who Received the Letter

1. Notice in verse 2 that the letter is addressed to a specific congregation. Identify the church and locate its city on the map (on p. vii). As the capital of the Roman province of Achaia, Corinth was an important city. It was located on a narrow neck of land between the Gulf of Corinth to its southeast and the Saronic Gulf to its northwest. Being on a major trade route brought prosperity to the city. Even though many of its people were well educated and many were rich, the city was known far and wide as a sinful place. The wickedness of its neighbors caused many problems for the Corinthian congregation.

2. Look up Acts 18:1-18 and note what it tells us about Corinth.

3. Why is it important to know who is being addressed in the letter?

_____

_____

_____

Note that Paul addressed his letter to the "church of God." The Greeks used the word *church* to refer to any assembly of people. It was often used in the Greek world for a city council, a group which had power in the affairs of government. Paul also used the word *church* not only to mean an assembly of people, but by adding the words *of God* to show that it was different than a political group.

C. Greeting
1. Read verse 3 and note the following words: *grace, peace, God our Father, the Lord, Jesus Christ.*

This became the typical Christian greeting. "Grace" resembles the usual Greek salutation, and "peace" the usual Hebrew greeting. This form is found in almost every letter in the New Testament. (See Rom. 1:7; 2 Cor. 1:2; Gal. 1:3.)

Grateful words filled with concern: 1:4-9
This is the second part of the introduction to the Corinthian letter. First Corinthians, like many of Paul's New Testament letters, includes some form of thanksgiving in its earliest parts. Note that Paul's thanksgiving reflects the concerns faced by the congregation to which he is writing. (See the introductions to the letters to the Romans, 1 Thessalonians, Philippians, Philemon, and Colossians.)

1. What is important about the fact that Paul thanks God for the Corinthians?

_____

2. As you work through the letter, you will notice changes in Paul's mood. Try to remain aware of these throughout each session. What is Paul's mood as he begins this letter (in v. 4)?

3. Beginning with verse 5, Paul names the gifts which God has given to the Corinthians. In what two special ways were the Corinthians enriched or blessed?

4. Chapters 12—14 show that even though the Corinthians had many spiritual gifts, they had many problems because they did not use their gifts in the right way.
According to verse 7, the Corinthians did not lack any spiritual gift. What do you think Paul meant by this?

5. Even though Paul's letter contains much criticism of the Corinthian congregation, the prayer in verses 4-9 sets the tone for the corrections he will call for. It sets his criticism in the context of love.
Do you describe your congregation in this way when you start out to talk about its faults? If you were to write a letter to your congregation, what would the introduction include? Would it sound like Paul's? How would it be different?

6 / HAVE THE MIND OF CHRIST

Cross of Christ emptied of its power: 1:10-17
Verse 9 completes Paul's introduction to the letter. Paul begins this next section of the letter by describing a basic problem within the Corinthian church.

1. What kinds of things has Paul heard about the Corinthian congregation?

2. Through whom did Paul receive such news?

3. In what way, according to verse 12, were the people divided? Whom were the Corinthians following?

(a) _____

(b) _____

(c) _____

(d) _____

4. Is your congregation divided? Do some people follow different leaders in the church? Do some give their main loyalty to radio or television preachers? Do they take their cues from persons outside the church?

5. What would Paul's words in this section mean for your church?

6. List the main points of Paul's argument in verses 13-17. What is the chief idea he wants to get across?

7. What, according to verse 17, is the connection between baptism and the gospel? How does baptism fit into Paul's overall argument in verses 10-17?

Summary
In this lesson we have seen that Paul wrote the letter of 1 Corinthians to a specific congregation and for a specific reason. In these first seventeen verses, Paul has barely touched the surface of the problems faced by the Corinthian church. The rest of his letter will go on to deal with a number of them in greater depth. The next lesson picks up the reason that the Corinthians were having so many problems: Paul accuses them of putting too much emphasis on human wisdom.

Session 2. Christ the power and wisdom of God

1 Corinthians 1:18-31

In Session 1 we looked at the opening of the Corinthian letter. We saw that Paul's writing style was like that of other first-century writers. We also learned that the Corinthian congregation faced divisions among its members.

In the next passage, Paul explains the cause of the church's problems. It seems the Corinthians were placing great emphasis on the importance of wisdom. Paul warns them that they are substituting "worldly wisdom" for "divine wisdom." In 1:18—2:16, Paul develops this contrast between worldly and godly wisdom.

The foolishness of what was preached: 1:18-25
Here Paul argues that the gospel contains not human wisdom but divine power.

1. In verse 18, Paul discusses the two ways of the "message of the cross":

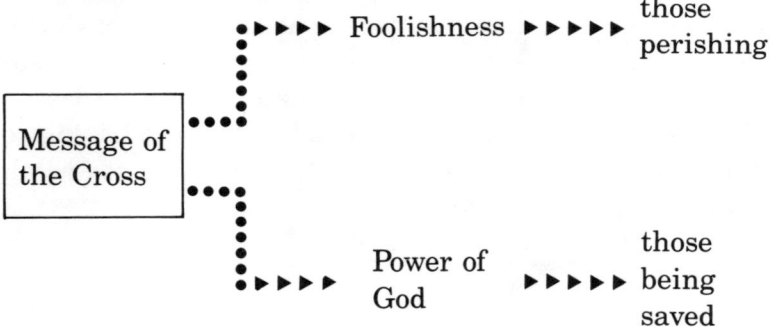

```
                          Foolishness  ▶▶▶▶  those
                                              perishing
  ┌──────────────┐
  │ Message of   │
  │ the Cross    │
  └──────────────┘
                          Power of      ▶▶▶▶  those
                          God                 being
                                              saved
```

Read verses 18-25. From this first reading, what seems to be the difference between "wisdom" and the "message of the cross?"

_____

_____

_____

The next four items will help us understand the meaning of "foolishness" and "wisdom." Study numbers 2-5 below as a unit.

2. Write out the meaning of *foolishness* and *wisdom* according to the way Paul seems to be using them.

Foolishness: _____

_____

Wisdom: _____

_____

3. How can you tell that Paul does not imply that foolish shows a lack of learning or that wise means being educated?

_____

_____

_____

4. How can you tell that wisdom and foolishness do not refer to some natural gift?

_____

_____

_____

5. Think of someone you know quite well whom you would consider wise.

10 / HAVE THE MIND OF CHRIST

(a) What is it about that person that makes you think of him or her as wise?

_____

_____

_____

(b) Would Paul—according to the verses here—have considered this person to be wise? Why or why not?

_____

_____

6. In verse 19, Paul inserts a verse from the Old Testament. Note the words "it is written" at the beginning of verse 19. This is Paul's usual way of introducing Old Testament quotations. You will find this same formula used again in other parts of the Corinthian letter.

In this case, Paul cites Isaiah 29:14. Isaiah's words were spoken to the people of Judah who were facing an invasion by Assyria. Read Isaiah 29:13-14 in order to understand its meaning in the Old Testament. How did conditions in Judah in Old Testament times compare with what Paul saw happening in the Corinthian church?

_____

_____

_____

7. In verse 20, Paul argues by using some questions. How does he use these questions to make his point?

_____

_____

_____

8. In this entire section, and especially in verses 21-24, Paul contrasts the foolishness or wisdom of humankind

SESSION 2 / 11

with the foolishness or wisdom of God. In doing so, he clearly outlines—most sharply in verse 25—a pattern showing how each item is higher or lower than another:

> the wisdom of God
> ▼
> the foolishness of God
> ▼
> the wisdom of man
> ▼
> the foolishness of man

In arguing this, Paul is dealing with a first-century belief known as Gnosticism. Gnostics believed that salvation came through knowledge (*gnosis*) or "wisdom." Paul disagrees. He says that the greatest "wisdom of man" is still only foolishness by God's standards.

Study Paul's argument in verse 21 as he begins to develop this thought. Jot down in your own words what he means by this verse.

_____

_____

_____

9. Verses 22-24 show how Jewish thinking differed from Greek thinking. In order to understand this difference, complete the following sentences based on these verses.

(a) The Jews looked for _____ which would prove the _____ of God.

(b) The Greeks looked for _____ which would prove the _____ of God.

10. Verse 22 gives us a hint as to why Paul deals with wisdom in this letter. The Greeks placed a lot of stress on human wisdom. They took great pride in the high marks their people had made in the field of learning through

persons such as Plato and Aristotle. They measured the new religion of Jesus Christ that Paul was presenting against their knowledge and wisdom. Paul tries to change this course of thinking by arguing that Christ is the "wisdom of God" (v. 24).

Paul also shows how the Jews differed. They had little interest in the wisdom of the Greeks. Rather, they looked for miracles which were a sign of the power of God. Paul, in the same breath as he tells the Greeks that Christ is the wisdom of God, also tells the Jews that Christ is the "power of God" (v. 24).

Are you more like the Jews or the Greeks?

(a) Are you impressed—as were the Jews—by power and by miracles? Before answering this question, list some of the gains made by various religious groups in recent years. Who has added the most members? Who has sent out the most missionaries? Who has started the most new programs? Who has built the finest buildings? How do you feel about these deeds? Would the Jews about whom Paul was talking have called these miracles and the power of God?

_____

_____

_____

(b) Are you impressed by ideas and by the use of words? Before answering this question, list some of the best slogans that you have heard in the last year, including words on posters, titles of sermons, titles of books, or special answers to hard questions. How do you feel about these ideas? Would the Greeks about whom Paul was talking have been impressed by this wisdom?

_____

_____

(c) Do you place more emphasis on signs or on wisdom? Why?

___

11. (a) What does Paul say to those who are looking for a visible sign of God's power?

___

(b) What does Paul say to those who want to have an explanation of God in wise words?

___

God chose the foolish things of the world: 1:26-31
Here Paul says even more about wisdom. He uses an example which comes close to home for the people of the Corinthian church, namely, their own lives.

1. In verse 26 Paul points to the members of the Corinthian church. What kind of people were in this congregation?

___

2. How do the people in the Corinthian church compare to the people in your congregation?

___

3. How do verses 26-31 fit into Paul's main argument begun in verse 18? In other words, why would Paul follow up his discussion in verses 18-25 by drawing attention to the backgrounds of the people in Corinth?

4. Take a moment to reflect for yourself on Paul's instruction in verse 26a: "think of what you were when you were called." Imagine yourself as a member of the Corinthian church. How would you have felt and what would you have thought about when you would have heard these words and the words in the following verses?

5. According to these verses, Paul was anxious to show the Corinthian people that their salvation—beginning with their call—did not come to them because they had earned it. What three pairs of opposites does Paul use in verses 27-28 to illustrate this point?

(a) _____

(b) _____

(c) _____

6. Notice what Paul says about "boasting" in this section (vv. 29 and 31). What does verse 31b ("Let him who

boasts boast in the Lord") mean? See also Jeremiah 9:23-24, which is the Old Testament source of this quotation.

7. The people of Corinth greatly stressed human wisdom. What do you see as the value of human wisdom? What are its limits?

Summary
This lesson has shown us why the church in Corinth was in trouble. Paul says its big problems are rooted in one bigger issue: the Corinthian Christians were making their own wisdom equal to God's wisdom. Sometimes they even put it ahead of God's wisdom.

In our next session, Paul continues his discussion about wisdom, adding an explanation of how God reveals his wisdom to us through the Spirit.

Session 3. But we have the mind of Christ

1 Corinthians 2:1-16

In our last session, we saw how Paul warned the Corinthian Christians against substituting worldly wisdom for divine wisdom. He discouraged them from placing too much emphasis on human wisdom.

In this session, we will see that 1 Corinthians 2 continues the discussion on the place of wisdom in the church. As Paul added to his thoughts on wisdom, he brought in the "wisdom of the Spirit [of God]" contrasting it with human wisdom.

Resting on the Spirit's power: 2:1-5
1. Read verses 1-5 and describe how Paul felt when he first came to Corinth.

2. What was the central message that Paul was trying to get across in his preaching to the Corinthians?

3. What did Paul preach about? How did he describe the style of his preaching?

4. Sum up the message, the manner, and the motive of Paul's preaching at the time that the Corinthian congregation was just beginning.

Message: _____

Manner: _____

Motive: _____

5. Paul described his preaching as a "demonstration of the Spirit's power" that was not supported by "wise and persuasive words" (v. 4). Which of these is important to you when you hear a sermon? How do you recognize them?

_____

_____

6. In verse 5, Paul put his finger on the cause of the problem in the Corinthian church. This verse states his goal for the church, but the exact opposite happened. Write out Paul's goal and then write out what really happened.

Paul's goal: _____

What really happened: _____

7. Read verse 5 again, and consider on what *your* faith is based. Write it down and explain why.

_____

_____

_____

Expressing spiritual truths in spiritual words: 2:6-16

In this section, Paul claims that the gospel contains true wisdom, but that it is a wisdom understood only by the "mature" (v. 6). The gospel contains not the wisdom of the world but the wisdom of God. The wisdom of the world cannot see either God or the fruits of God's wisdom, while the wisdom of God is said to be wisdom hidden in mystery. The source of this revealed wisdom of God is the "Spirit of God" (vv. 10-16).

1. In 2:6-7, Paul speaks about the two kinds of wisdom. Name these two types.

(a) _____

_____

(b) _____

_____

2. What would you see as the difference between these two types of wisdom?

_____

_____

3. In verse 6 Paul refers to the mature and to the "rulers of this age." Paul contrasts mature with "infants." (See 1 Cor. 3:1-4.) Mature refers to the fully developed Christian, a state which the Corinthian Christians had not yet reached.

SESSION 3 / 19

The rulers of this age are the earthly Jewish and Roman rulers. Verse 8 tells us that these rulers were the ones who lacked an understanding of Christ and the ones who finally crucified him. Answer the following questions by referring to verses 6-8:

(a) What type of wisdom does Paul find in those who are mature?

___

___

(b) What type of wisdom does he find in the rulers of the age?

___

___

(c) What type of wisdom, do you think, Paul would say that the rulers of *our* age have?

___

___

4. In verses 7-9, Paul describes God's wisdom as "hidden" and as a "secret." This idea of the mysterious implies a secret that humans cannot discover by themselves but which God reveals as God chooses. God's wisdom is hidden in that it is only revealed to faith, and has nothing to do with persuasive words or human wisdom.

Describe as fully as you can this secret wisdom that Paul talks about. To help with this, check 1 Corinthians 4:1; 13:2; 14:2; Colossians 1:26; 2:2; and 4:3.

___

___

___

5. Write out in your own words what Paul is saying in verses 7-9.

_____

_____

_____

Note that verse 9 is an Old Testament quotation (from Isa. 64:4). Paul begins the verse by saying "it is written," which was his usual way of introducing Scripture. Paul had a habit of making his point and then quoting an Old Testament passage to confirm it. The main reason for this quote is to prove that the gospel is a fulfillment of the promises to Israel.

6. Beginning with the second part of verse 10, Paul speaks about the source which makes us able to understand the mystery of God. We see that true wisdom is given us through the Spirit.

How does a person get to know the secret or hidden wisdom which Paul mentions in verse 7? See especially verse 10.

_____

_____

_____

7. In verse 12 Paul speaks of two different kinds of spirits. What are they?

(a) _____

_____

(b) _____

_____

8. What does the Spirit of God help us to understand?

_____

_____

9. According to verse 13, what work does the Spirit of God do?

10. Note how these verses relate to verses 6 and 7:

Wisdom of this Age (verse 6)	Hidden Wisdom of God (verse 7)
▼	▼
Spirit of the World (verse 12)	Spirit of God (verse 12)

Consider for a moment how these two pairs are related to each other.

11. Does this section seem to say that it is possible or impossible to know anything about God without the Spirit? Why?

12. Verses 12-14 also say that the Spirit of God is the source of spiritual insight.
(a) What happens to the person without the Spirit?

(b) How is that different from what happens to the spiritual person?

(c) How can we tell the difference between those who have the Spirit and those who do not? What guides did Paul give us for making this judgment?

13. In verse 15 we read that "the spiritual man makes judgments about all things, but he himself is not subject to any man's judgment." This verse shows that the spiritual person tests all things, both secular and spiritual. Because the spiritual person has received the Spirit, this person is able to judge all things from this new, Spirit-filled point of view. This verse also shows that the spiritual person, insofar as that person reflects the Spirit of God, cannot be judged by others.

Does your congregation practice verse 15? In what ways does it? In what ways does it not?

14. In verse 16, Paul quotes Isaiah 40:13. (The word *mind* likely means the same as the word *Spirit*.)

Keeping this in mind, what does it mean to "have the mind of Christ?"

15. An important idea in the Christian teaching is the Trinity (God consisting of three-persons-in-one: the Father, the Son, the Holy Spirit). In this letter, Paul speaks about the way Jesus is related to God (1:18—2:5), and about the way the Spirit fits into this picture (2:1-16). See what you can learn from 1:18—2:16 about Paul's understanding of the Trinity.

Summary
In chapter 2 Paul compares the way of the Spirit—which reveals the wisdom of God—with the way of the world. While the way of the world is followed by those outside the church, Paul says that the wisdom of God is accepted by mature Christians. Mature Christians are also described as spiritual persons, having the mind of Christ.

Paul saw the Corinthians' use of different kinds of wisdom as the root of many of their congregational problems. Having ended his discussion of wisdom in chapter 2, Paul turned to the many issues that developed in the church, beginning in chapter 3 with the problem of divisions in the congregation.

Session 4. God's fellow workers are only servants

1 Corinthians 3:1-23

We have already seen (in 1 Cor. 1:10-17) the divisions among the members of the Corinthian congregation. One of the problems facing the congregation was that they saw the different workers (Apollos, Cephas, Paul) as rival party leaders. Paul explains that the cause of this division is due to too much emphasis on the person proclaiming the gospel and not enough stress on the gospel itself.

In Session 3 we heard Paul say that the gospel was divine power, not human wisdom. He compared the different types of wisdom to show that true wisdom has its source in God and is revealed to people through the Spirit of God.

The thought that runs through chapter 3 is that apostles and teachers are agents through whom God works, and that the message (the gospel) is more important than the messengers bringing the gospel.

Dieting on milk instead of solid food: 3:1-4
In these verses, Paul refers back to the time when he first worked in Corinth. He compares the present state of the Corinthian Christians to the way they were when he first arrived in Corinth.

Paul says the Corinthians were young Christians when he first visited them, and as such they could not be treated as mature (spiritual) Christians. He goes on, however, to say that they are still immature (worldly) and that this failure to grow keeps them from understanding the deeper teachings that he would like to give them.

1. How does Paul describe the condition of the Corinthian Christians?

_____

_____

_____

2. According to verse 2, what has the lack of growth among the Christians of Corinth done to Paul's work?

_____

_____

3. Note that Paul fed them "milk" instead of "solid food." Milk, in this context, is that preaching which is directed toward those who are not spiritual. This would include preaching that is aimed especially at calling non-Christians to become followers of Christ.

Solid food represents the message for convinced Christians, going into the gospel in more depth.

(a) What is your understanding of the difference between feeding Christians milk and solid food?

_____

_____

_____

(b) How soon should young Christians progress from milk to solid food?

_____

_____

_____

(c) How does your congregation compare to the Corinthian congregation? Are you still infants in Christ? Does your diet consist of milk or solid food?

_____

_____

_____

4. In what ways does Paul show that the Corinthian Christians are still worldly?

(a) _____

_____

(b) _____

_____

(c) _____

_____

Note that Paul does not say that the members of the Corinthian congregation are unchanged people, but only that they *live* as those who are unchanged. In other words, he does not deny that they are Christians, but he scolds them for not walking according to the Spirit.

Moving from God's field to God's building: 3:5-17
The Corinthians were making too much of the different leaders within the congregation, each party glorifying its leader and bringing shame to Christ and to the gospel. In the following verses Paul says that apostles, though special in the work of the church, should not be idolized or singled out for special honor.

A. God makes things grow: 3:5-9
In these verses Paul points out that in the work of evangelizing Corinth and building the congregation in that city, he and Apollos were acting as agents of God.

1. Verse 5 defines the role of the agent of God. Who are the people identified as agents, and what is their function?

                Agent   Function

(a) _____   _____

(b) _____   _____

2. In verse 5 Paul refers to himself and Apollos as servants. The Greek word which is translated as "servants" *diakonoi* can also be translated as "deacons."

What do you think it means to be a servant, in the sense that Paul was also a servant?

_____

_____

Notice Paul's comment in verse 6. After asking "What ... is Apollos/Paul?" it seems the answer should be "Nothing." But Paul doesn't say that. In other words, the apostles are important, though only servants. Only when compared to God are they insignificant.

3. Paul uses two special metaphors (word pictures) in verses 6-9 to describe the work that he and Apollos were doing. Name these metaphors and list the people that are part of these word pictures.

_____

_____

_____

4. Verse 6 describes the tasks that Paul and Apollos performed in Corinth. What does verse 6 tell us about who began, and who later developed, the Corinthian church? See also Acts 18:24-28.

_____

5. Verse 7 says that neither the planter nor the waterer are important. The only thing special about Paul and Apollos is that God accepted their works and worked through them. Instead of focusing on the human servants, the attention of the Corinthians should have been turned toward God.
Who are the planters and waterers in your congregation? How much honor do you give to each?

6. In verse 8 Paul notes the unity between the planter and the waterer; both have a common purpose. Neither can succeed without the work of the other. Paul says he and Apollos are not competing with each other. They have the same goal in mind.
(a) According to verse 8, how do the work of the planter and the waterer go together?

(b) How do the workers in your congregation support each other?

B. Building on the foundation: 3:10-15
In these verses, Paul moves from describing the Corinthian Christians as God's field to God's building. The

thoughts in these verses really repeat those in the verses that have gone before.

1. How does Paul describe his work as a builder in Corinth?

_____

_____

_____

2. Note the words "each one should be careful how he builds" in verse 10. These words bring out the thought of individual and personal responsibility. All persons should be careful in the way they build upon the foundation.

To whom is Paul referring when he says *"someone else is building on [the foundation that I laid]"* and *"each one should be careful how he builds"* (v. 10, italics supplied)?

_____

_____

Paul describes himself as the expert builder and speaks about having laid a foundation. Then he goes on to identify (v. 11) exactly what the foundation is: Jesus Christ. Paul probably says this because some Christians, possibly in Corinth, were misinterpreting the words of Jesus in Matthew 16:18, where Jesus says that he will build his church on Simon Peter, the rock. Paul here says that the foundation of the church is always Jesus Christ, not any apostle.

3. Write down the various materials which may be used for building that Paul lists in verse 12. Note that there are two classes of material:

(a) Better material:

    (i) _____

    (ii) _____

(iii) _____

(b) Worse material:

(i) _____

(ii) _____

(iii) _____

People can use different materials when building on the foundation. Verse 13 says that at some point the material and the workmanship will be tested. Paul speaks of this happening on "the Day." He does not need to explain what he means by this, since any Christian of Jewish background would know that this referred to "the Day of the Lord," a common Old Testament idea. (For an example, see Amos 5:18-20.)

In Paul's thought, on the Day of the Lord, our secrets will be judged (Rom. 2:16). Therefore, any faulty workmanship, though built on solid foundation, will be destroyed. The idea that testing would happen by fire was a common one. In the case of the building illustration that Paul is using, fire fits well.

4. (a) What things are being built on the church's foundation in our day? Following Paul's illustration, what kind of materials are represented by these actions?

_____

_____

(b) Which of these materials will remain standing when tested?

_____

_____

(c) Note that the *quality* of each person's work is stressed, while no mention is made of *quantity*. What do we tend to emphasize in our day: quality or quantity? Why?

5. (a) If the quality of a person's work survives the test, what is the outcome (v. 14)?

(b) If the quality of a person's work does not survive the test, what is the outcome (v. 15)? Does Paul imply that people may be saved even though their contribution to the church may not be permanent? How?

What exactly is Paul trying to say by his metaphor (word picture) in verses 10-15? A good possibility is that he is addressing Jewish Christians (that's why he speaks about such things as "the Day," which persons of Jewish background would have understood), who were trying to build their old Jewish ideas (separation from Gentiles, legalism, and so on) into the church. (See, for example, Gal. 2:11-14.)

Paul tells them that such a system will be destroyed, although they themselves will not be excluded from salvation because of it. Verse 15, however, adds that though such persons "will be saved," they will still suffer pain and loss, and be scarred by the experience.

6. In summary, what is the main point of verses 10-15?

7. Notice the straightforwardness—which could be interpreted as pride—with which Paul speaks about his own ministry. He refers to himself as God's worker, God's planter (v. 6), as an expert builder (v. 10), and so on, while those he is addressing are God's field (v. 9), infants who need milk instead of solids (vv. 1-2). How do you suppose Paul would have been received by someone to whom he had spoken in this way? How do we react today when someone speaks to us in such a tone? Why?

C. God's Spirit in our temple: 3:16-17
The picture that Paul used in verses 10-15 apparently drew him off in another direction. In speaking of Jesus as a foundation, and about the building erected on that foundation, Paul is reminded of some thoughts about the temple of God.
  1. What is the illustration that Paul gives in verse 16?

  2. What does it mean to be God's temple?

  3. Does the "you" of verse 16 (God's Spirit lives in *you*) refer to the congregation in Corinth as a whole, or to the individual members of the church? In other words, is

God's Spirit present in each individual or in the church?

_____

_____

_____

4. In verse 17, Paul speaks of the chance that the church (God's temple) might be destroyed. Yet, in Matthew 16:18, Jesus says the church will endure. No doubt the best way to square these two statements with each other is to assume that Jesus was speaking about the church as a whole, whereas Paul was referring to the local congregation. Though the church as a whole may not be destroyed, the individual congregation may be. For this reason, Paul is sending out a warning.

(a) What kinds of things can destroy a congregation?

_____

_____

(b) Give an example of something which you have done or not done which has hurt the congregation?

_____

_____

_____

D. No more boasting: 3:18-23
These verses sum up what Paul has already discussed earlier in his letter to the Corinthians, namely, the difference between wisdom and foolishness.

1. Looking back over chapters 1—3, what do you think Paul means in verses 18-20 by things that persons allow to deceive them?

_____

_____

2. It seems that the Corinthians were struggling to be both members of a congregation of Christians and to be wise in the ways of the world at the same time. Is this something that your congregation struggles with today? In what way?

3. Read verse 21.
(a) What does "boasting about men" mean?

(b) In what way were the Corinthian Christians guilty of such "boasting about men"?

(c) In what way are we like the Corinthian Christians when it comes to boasting about others? How do we make idols out of particular church members, leaders, or preachers?

4. What is the main point of verses 21b-23?

5. According to chapter 3, list some of the things which you learned about leaders in the church. What is their place? What should they do? How should they act?

_____

_____

_____

Summary
In chapter 3, Paul has tried to put into the correct order of importance (1) the gospel, and (2) those who bring the gospel. For Paul the gospel is all-important. The apostles who bring the "good news" are significant because of their message, but they should still be regarded as mere persons. The Corinthians, apparently, were beginning to idolize their human leaders, and Paul criticizes them for doing so. Christians are to remember that apostles are only important when they point to God.

Having said all of that, Paul in chapter 4 goes on to say something about the life of an apostle, and to appeal to the Corinthians for unity in their congregation.

Session 5. An apostle and parent worth imitating

1 Corinthians 4:1-21

In chapter 3 Paul said that the Corinthian Christians' quarrels were a sign of their spiritual immaturity. He scolded them for being worldly and for remaining infants in Christ.

Paul also made it clear that he and Apollos were both servants of Christ. Even though they had individual tasks, they were working with the same goals in mind.

In chapter 4 Paul comes to the high point of his appeal for unity among the Corinthian Christians, and concludes his writing regarding strife in the Corinthian congregation.

Servants of Christ entrusted with secret things: 4:1-5

In this section, Paul concludes that leaders like him are ministers of Jesus Christ and stewards of God's "secret things." He encourages the Corinthians to have the right attitude toward apostles and teachers.

1. How should the Corinthian Christians regard their spiritual leaders (v. 1)?

2. Note the phrase "servant of Christ" (v. 1). This means that Christ is the master of their spiritual leaders. Paul means that none of the leaders serving the Co-

rinthian church can claim anything for themselves except the honor as Christ's workers. Paul stresses this point because the Corinthians had treated their leaders as lords.

Also take note of the phrase "the secret things of God" (v. 1). What does it mean to be a "servant of Christ entrusted with the secret things of God?"

_____

_____

_____

3. What, according to verse 2, is the most important requirement for a servant of Christ?

_____

_____

4. What words are often used today to describe a minister of the church? How do words like *servant* or *steward* (someone entrusted with something by God) fit in with this model of a minister?

_____

_____

_____

5. How does Paul feel about being judged by the Corinthians?

_____

_____

_____

6. Read verses 3-5 again and note that there are three different types of judgment mentioned in this section:
  (a) verse 3 speaks of a judgment passed by others;
  (b) verse 4 makes reference to the judgment of one's own conscience; and

(c) verses 4 and 5 include a discussion of the Lord's judgment.

List, if you can, personal examples where you:
(a) were judged by others.

_____

_____

(b) faced judgment by your own conscience.

_____

_____

(c) were judged by God.

_____

_____

(d) Which of the above three judgments are you most concerned about?

_____

_____

_____

7. Notice (in v. 4) that a clear conscience does not mean innocence. What do you think is the role of a person's (of your!) conscience?

_____

_____

_____

8. Another way of saying that there are three types of judgment (as in #6 above) is to say that Christians are *accountable* to three parties:

```
┌──────────┐           ┌──────────┐
│  other   │           │          │
│  people  │           │   God    │
└──────────┘           └──────────┘
     ▲                      ▲
     ·                      ·
     ·                      ·
     ·   ┌───────────┐      ·
     ···▶│ Christian │◀··· ·
         └───────────┘
               ▲
               ·
               ▼
         ┌───────────┐
         │   self    │
         │(conscience)│
         └───────────┘
```

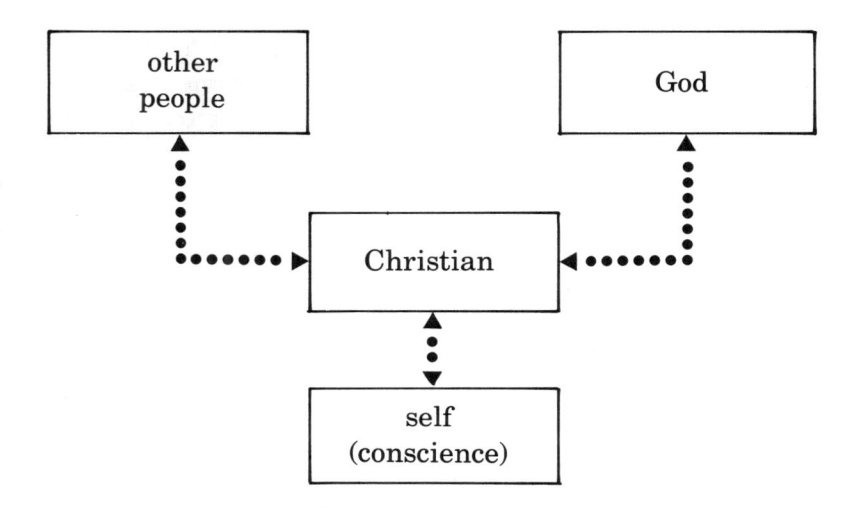

9. Rank in order of importance these three groups: to which of them do you feel most accountable? least accountable?

(a) _____

(b) _____

(c) _____

Most accountable? _____

Least accountable? _____

10. Consider how you as an individual are accountable to these three groups. How does your congregation use these three sets of checks and balances in the church?

_____

_____

_____

We are fools for Christ but you are so wise: 4:6-13

In this paragraph Paul returns to the idea he has been talking about through most of the letter up to this point: the Corinthians must not exaggerate the importance of such leaders as Paul and Apollos. Paul points the Corinthians away from loyalties for such different leaders to a central loyalty to Christ because everyone must answer to Christ. The emphasis is not on the apostle/teacher but on the Master whom the leader serves.

1. Why has Paul used Apollos and himself as illustrations here?

_____

_____

_____

2. The word used by Paul which is translated "what is written" (v. 6) is a formula used regularly to introduce quotes from Scripture (the Old Testament). (See the note in Session 2, p. 10 above.) For Paul, "Do not go beyond what is written" means "Do not go beyond/do not ignore the teachings of Scripture [for Paul, Scripture referred simply to the Old Testament]; the Jewish Scriptures are not to be discarded by the church." Paul may also intend to apply this statement to the passages of Scripture that he has quoted so far in his letter.

Can we take this instruction of Paul seriously? Do we tend to "go beyond what is written (in Scripture—the Old Testament)"? If so, how?

_____

_____

_____

3. What three questions does Paul ask in verse 7?

(a) _____

(b) _____

(c) _____

4. What answers does Paul seem to expect to his three questions in verse 7? How does he get his point across that way?

_____

_____

5. In verse 7 Paul asks his readers "For who makes you different from anyone else?" In other words, the Corinthians were thinking themselves to be different from others. In verse 8 Paul begins to use strong satire. (Satire is a form of speech that uses a serious tone of voice to make fun of some human weakness.) Paul says, in effect, "Yes, you are different all right. But not necessarily in a good way."

Carefully read through verses 8-13. Jot down what Paul means by his use of satire (especially in v. 8).

_____

_____

Paul is making several points in verse 8. Two of the key ones are: (1) in saying "you have become kings," Paul means "you have come to reign over the kingdom that *you* wanted." In other words, the kingdom that you are kings over is not the kingdom of God. And, he adds, almost as an afterthought: "and that [you did] without us!" (2) The second key thought that Paul introduces in verse 8, and continues to develop in verses 9-13, is that an apostle is really the opposite of an earthly king.

6. What does Paul say about the life of an apostle in verse 9?

_____

_____

_____

7. In verse 10 Paul proceeds with the contrast between himself, his fellow missionaries, and the self-satisfied Corinthians. Paul uses irony to show that he has become foolish by worldly standards in order to be wise in a Christlike sense, and that the Corinthians' wisdom is more like worldly wisdom. (Irony is a way of speaking in which the tone of voice shows that the words spoken are meant to have a meaning opposite to the usual meaning of those words.)

List three ways in which Paul compares himself and the other apostles with the Corinthian Christians.

(a) We are _____

You are _____

(b) We are _____

You are _____

(c) We are _____

You are _____

8. Verses 11-13 describe the sufferings of the apostles. List the kind of things that they experienced.

_____

_____

Compare the list above with Paul's experiences in Acts 9:15, 16, 23-25; 14:19-20; 16:22-24; 17:32.

_____

_____

9. What do verses 12-13 tell us about the kind of spirit with which the apostles met opposition to their work? List the three examples given in this passage.

_____

The behavior that Paul describes in this verse recalls the teachings of Jesus. Compare the ideas found in this verse with the following sections of the Sermon on the Mount: Matthew 5:5, 10-12, 44; Luke 6:21-23, 35.

10. In verse 12, Paul says, "We work hard with our own hands." This may be a reference to Paul's practice of supporting himself by tentmaking (Acts 18:3) without appealing to others for support.
How are needs of ministers and missionaries cared for in your church?

11. Briefly list in two separate columns the comparisons that Paul makes between the apostles' situation and that of the Corinthian Christians (vv. 8-13).

Corinthian Christians	Apostles' Situation

12. Which column does your life compare to most closely?

_____

13. What kind of struggles are apostles of today facing?

_____

_____

14. Do Christians today face as many problems as the apostles in Paul's day did? Why? Or, why not?

_____

_____

_____

Not to shame but to warn: 4:14-21
Paul now brings his letter's lengthy opening thoughts (chaps. 1—4) to a close. Verses 14-21 form the closing paragraph of the first part of his letter.

1. So far in the letter, Paul has said a number of things to the Corinthians which probably left them feeling ashamed. Yet Paul now states most firmly that that was not his purpose in writing the letter. What was Paul's intent for this letter (v. 14)?

_____

_____

2. Even though the Corinthian Christians had many teachers, Paul was more than a teacher to them. What was his special connection with them?

_____

3. Because Paul is their "spiritual father" he encourages the Corinthians, in verse 16, to_____

Paul has described for the Corinthians an apostle whose life is made up of suffering and service to others. This kind of apostleship is based on the example of Christ's life. Just as Paul, the apostle, followed Jesus, so Paul urges the Corinthians to follow their spiritual father.

4. How does 4:16 fit in with what Paul has said up to this point in this letter? Before answering this question, review especially 1:12-15; 3:4-6.

5. Why did Paul send Timothy to the Corinthians?

6. What does Paul say about Timothy (v. 17)?

7. In verse 18 Paul says that the behavior of some of the Corinthian Christians shows that they think he is not going to return again. In other words, when his back is turned they do as they please.

(a) Does the presence of certain people have an effect on your personal behavior? In what way?

(b) Should you act differently depending on who is watching you?

8. What does verse 20 mean when it says that "the kingdom of God is not a matter of *talk* but of *power*" (italics added)?

9. Would you say that your church places more emphasis on talk or on power?

10. Paul ends this section by saying that when he comes to visit the Corinthians, the attitude with which he will come will depend on the attitude of the people in the church.

If Paul were to visit your congregation today, what would be his response to the actions and attitudes of the people within your congregation? Would Paul need to come with "a whip" or would he come to you with a "gentle spirit"?

11. List two or three things you have learned about leadership while working through this chapter.

_____

_____

_____

12. Chapters 1—4 form the first major division of 1 Corinthians. What would you say has been Paul's chief concern so far?

_____

_____

_____

Summary

In chapter 4 Paul has continued to urge the Corinthians not to exaggerate the importance of human leaders such as himself and Apollos. At the same time, he discusses the life of an apostle, claiming it to be more Christlike than the lifestyle of the Corinthians.

Chapter 4 ends the discussion of disunity within the Corinthian church. Throughout this section, Paul has shown that he is dealing with a congregation that prefers the wisdom of the world more than the wisdom of Christ. This outlook on life has caused a lot of problems within the church.

All through 1 Corinthians it is clear that Paul is deeply concerned about the spirit, the well-being, and the mission of the church that he has founded. He writes with the conviction that those who are betraying and destroying the cause need to change their ways. So, he goes on in chapter 5 to a discussion of discipline in the church.

Session 6. Eat not with an immoral brother

1 Corinthians 5:1-13

The letter to the church at Corinth deals with many different problems within the church. So far, in chapters 1—4, Paul has spent most of his time focusing on disunity in the congregation. The second section of the letter, chapters 5—7, deals with ethical problems such as sexual immorality, taking each other to court, and questions pertaining to marriage. These chapters open another window into the life of the Corinthian congregation.

The problem dealt with in chapter 5 is sexual immorality. It will be easier to understand this problem once we are aware of the moral background and reputation of the people of Corinth.

Generally speaking, many of the people living in Corinth saw no connection between religious faith and everyday life. Religion in Corinth meant the worship of gods who set examples of sensual pleasure and self-indulgence. Converts to Christianity coming from such a background did not easily shed all of their former values and their outlook on life. That's why so many struggles surfaced.

Worse than pagan immorality: 5:1-5
1. What report had Paul heard about the Corinthian congregation (v. 1)?

SESSION 6 / 49

2. What does verse 1 imply about the seriousness of this action?

What is the act reported in verse 1? "A man has his father's wife" is rather unclear. Since Paul does refer to this as adultery, the father was probably not living or else had divorced his wife. Secondly, Paul does not describe the situation as incest, so it is unlikely that the woman was the offender's mother. The most logical conclusion is that the woman involved was probably the offender's stepmother.

3. What does Paul think of the attitude that the church has taken toward the situation?

4. What attitude should the people of Corinth have taken?

5. Verse 2 tells us that only one of the offenders was to be disciplined. Which one is it?

6. Why is only the one person mentioned as needing disciplining?

Paul seems as concerned about the community's attitude toward the sinner's conduct as he is about the sinner himself. In 1:2, Paul spoke of the church at Corinth as "sanctified in Christ Jesus and called to be holy." As such a community, they should discourage immoral activity among members of their church.

7. Considering the marks of the Corinthian congregation that you have discovered so far, compare your congregation to the church in Corinth.

(a) Would Paul be shocked by any activity present in your church? What kind of things would shock him?

(b) What is your congregation's attitude toward the actions of its members? In what ways are you different from or similar to the Corinthians in this regard?

8. In verse 3 Paul says that even though he is not present at Corinth in body he is there in spirit. This is to explain his feeling of oneness with the congregation even though he is not physically present. What action has Paul taken, saying he would have done the same had he been present?

9. In verse 4 Paul seems to envision a church meeting at Corinth. He cannot be present in body himself, but he can be present in spirit. Paul plans to make his contribution to the meeting through the Christians' reflection on what they can remember of his conviction, his character, and what they know of his thoughts in the present matter.

According to verse 4, under whose authority are the Corinthian Christians to meet?

───

───

Verse 5 contains Paul's recommended course of action that the Corinthians are encouraged to take. This verse, however, is hard to understand and has caused a great deal of difficulty in interpretation. Let us look closely at the problem phrases:

(a) "Hand this man over to Satan." On the surface, these six words can appear to mean that the church is to voluntarily turn a Christian over to Satan for permanent destruction. This surface-level interpretation, however, is faulty for several reasons: (i) such a Christian has already turned himself or herself over to Satan, and the church is therefore only recognizing formally what has in fact already occurred; (ii) secondly, the aim of such "turning over to Satan" is not for permanent destruction, but is rather with the hope of the final salvation of the person. In other words, it is an act done out of deep Christian love. Satan is here used only as a tool to further Christ's way. Satan's realm is understood as the arena *outside* the church, just as Christ is the ruler *in* the church.

(b) "So that the sinful nature [body/flesh] may be destroyed." Paul's Greek word may mean either body/flesh or the sinful nature. Paul implies such meanings in other places, such as Romans 7:5. For Paul, the body/flesh, in both the Romans and the Corinthian passages, is a source of moral evil and connected in the Corinthian verse to sexual immorality. Paul sees that through sexual immorality, the sinful nature (flesh) dominates the person. And Paul, convinced that the flesh is a source of evil, or at least an arena in which Satan could torment people (e.g., 2 Cor. 12:7), believes it better to save the person at the expense of the "sinful nature [the body]."

Notice that in saying this, Paul is making a fundamental distinction between the "person" and the "body." The body does not need to be spared; the person to whom the body belongs must be saved. (For a discussion of the body in the resurrection see 1 Cor. 15:35-41.)

(c) The last phrase of verse 5 states that "his spirit [may be] saved on the day of the Lord." For a note on the "Day (of the Lord)" see Session 4, page 30. That the spirit be saved was Paul's final hope. He hoped that the destruction of the sinful nature would finally gain the salvation of the person. Thus, the main reason for correcting the person was to save that person's spirit.

10. Sum up the action that Paul thinks should take place within the church in dealing with the erring person.

11. What is the main intent in excommunicating the erring person? Is Paul's bigger concern for the salvation of the individual or for the purity of the church?

12. Was Paul's proposal a wise course of action? Why?

13. Ways of dealing with sin in the congregation.
(a) Look up Matthew 18:15-19. Write its meaning here.

_____

_____

(b) How does Matthew 18:15-19 compare to 1 Corinthians 5:1-5?

_____

_____

14. Paul felt he needed to deal with problems within the church.
(a) In what ways is church discipline practiced within your congregation? Give some specific examples.

_____

_____

(b) Do you, as an individual, feel a sense of responsibility for the actions of other members in your congregation, or do you take the attitude that it is none of your business?

_____

_____

(c) What kind of things could the church do to encourage a higher standard of commitment among its members to each other?

_____

15. Paul uses discipline not as judgment, but for the purpose of redemption. How does this compare with the type of church discipline that you are familiar with? Are you more concerned to rid the church of a troublemaker or to help the person?

16. If an offender does not repent after withdrawing from the church, what else can the congregation do?

Be the yeastless bread of sincerity and truth: 5:6-8
In verses 6-8 Paul wants the church to take the advice given in verses 3-5 and do something about sin within the church. He points to the offender as a sign of impurity for the entire church. If the congregation refuses to act, it is possible that this sinful example could spread and infect the whole church.

Paul uses the imagery of the Passover to show how urgent it is to remove evil from the church. During the Passover, which was the celebration of the Jews' deliverance from Egyptian captivity (Exod. 12:29-51), the people cleaned out all the old leaven. The act of throwing out the old leaven in the Jewish celebration marked Israel's break with their life in Egypt.

1. In verse 6 Paul says, "Don't you know that a little yeast works through the whole batch of dough?"
   (a) To what does "little yeast" refer?

(b) To what could "whole batch of dough" refer?

2. The thrust of verse 7 is that the church must *exercise* discipline in order to maintain its purity.
(a) What action does Paul encourage the people to take?

(b) What effect will this action have on the congregation?

The last part of verse 7 refers to Christ as the Passover lamb who has been sacrificed. The great theme of Passover was deliverance. The historic deliverance from Egypt was remembered as a past event, enjoyed as a present fact, and greeted as a continuing experience. In the same way, Christ as the Lamb of God sums up God's action for the deliverance of his people: past, present, and future.
3. (a) In verse 8a, Paul encourages the Christians to do away with the "old yeast" in their congregation. To what does the old yeast refer?

(b) In verse 8b, Paul encourages them to live like "bread without yeast." To what does he compare the bread without yeast?

4. If Paul were to write to your congregation would he have to encourage you to get rid of old yeast? Give some examples?

5. In one or two sentences, sum up what Paul has said to the Corinthians in verses 6-8.

Expel the wicked man: 5:9-13
In this passage Paul says that in this world it is impossible to avoid mixing with immoral people. He does not expect the Corinthians to remove themselves completely from society. Living within the world, however, does not mean that a person has to be a part of immoral patterns of life found in the world. Paul makes it quite clear that if people call themselves Christians but deny this claim by their behavior, then severe action must be taken to deal with the situation. In other words, Paul is saying that Christians need to associate with people of the world. At the same time, Christians must follow a different ethic and need to have their behavior challenged if it too closely identifies with the world.

1. (a) In the Greek, "I have written you" (v. 9) clearly means "I wrote you." In other words, "In a previous letter I said . . ." What were Paul's instructions in his earlier letter (v. 9)?

(b) What Paul had written in his former letter had apparently been misunderstood. What does he say in verse 10 to make his meaning more clear?

(c) What does Paul then add in verse 11?

(d) What is the difference between what Paul is saying in verse 10 and verse 11? What groups are contrasted in verses 10 and 11?

2. In these verses (9-11), we see that Paul is firm about keeping the world *out of* the church (he even goes as far as to say that a Christian should not eat with a proclaimed Christian who is acting immorally). But at the same time, he wants to keep the church *in* the world.

(a) What does it mean to keep the world out of the church?

(b) Why is it important to separate the church from the world?

(c) What does it mean to keep the church in the world?

(d) Why is it important to keep the church in the world?

3. Is Paul saying that the morals of the world (those outside the church) will always be immoral? Or, is it possible that the morals of the world would at times be at the same level as (or higher than!) the church's?

4. What do verses 12-13 say about judging (a) those outside the church, and (b) those inside the church?

5. Look back over chapter 5 once more. What is the main idea that Paul is trying to get across to his readers?

Summary

For Paul, the church is all important. It is essential that the church, consisting of the people of God, be holy. In order for the church to be holy, it must rid itself of all evil within it. The example that Paul uses in chapter 5 is the problem of sexual immorality in the Corinthian congregation. Any impurity, including sexual immorality, must be removed from the church. At the same time, the offender must be dealt with lovingly, so that the sinner may again be drawn into the fellowship.

Chapter 5 deals with the first of a number of specific problems in the Corinthian congregation. From this problem of sexual immorality in chapter 5, Paul goes on to the issue of how disputes are settled between Christians. Our next session takes us into Paul's discussion of lawsuits and the Christian.

Session 7. Honor God with your body

1 Corinthians 6:1-20

In chapter 5 Paul dealt with an act of immorality within the Corinthian church. He said that it was up to the people in the church to deal with the issue, and to do so in a redemptive way. The last verses of that chapter refer to judgment, and this brings Paul to a related matter which he discusses in the first part of chapter 6. Some of the Corinthians were taking each other to court, and Paul criticizes them for this. After inserting several paragraphs (vv. 1-11) regarding lawsuits, he returns to the theme of church discipline in relation to sexual conduct (vv. 12-20).

Disputes among the saints: 6:1-8
Paul is upset with the Corinthians' use of lawsuits for two reasons: (1) Christians should not need to take their disputes to someone outside their own circles (vv. 1-6), never mind that (2) Christians should not have such disputes at all in the first place (vv. 7-8).

1. Read verse 1 carefully. Notice Paul's use of the words *ungodly* and *saints*. Neither word implies any moral (good/bad) judgment. Rather, *saints* describes those Christians within the congregation, and *ungodly* refers to the non-Christians outside the congregation. Paul isn't saying that Christians are better people than non-Christians, nor that secular (Roman) people would

not give fair settlements to Christian disputes, but only that issues between Christians should be settled by Christians.

2. In verse 2 Paul speaks about the saints judging the world. Paul may be taking this from Daniel 7:22, where judgment is given to the "saints of the Most High." The reference is to a final act of judging, which the Jews of Daniel's time expected in the "last days."

The first part of verse 3 has no parallel anywhere else in the Bible. Paul's comment on judging angels and on judging the world were to remind Christians that they were going to court about things that were trivial when compared to such bigger concerns. What is the main point that Paul is trying to get across in verses 2-3?

_____

_____

_____

3. The second part of verse 4 may be translated either as a command ("appoint as judges even men of little account in the church!") or as a question ("do you appoint as judges men of little account in the church?"). Carefully look at the meaning of verse 4 with both of these translations in mind. What, in verse 4, is Paul's advice regarding disputes among Christians?

_____

_____

_____

4. What does the practice of going before "unbelieving" judges imply concerning the ability of Christians (even those "of little account") as judges?

_____

_____

_____

5. What is the reason for Paul's disgust as expressed in verse 6?

_____

_____

6. The early Christians had inherited from the Jews a strong desire not to get a bad image with their unbelieving neighbors. Taking cases of "Christian versus Christian" into non-Christian courts, therefore, was a way of hanging out the Christians' dirty laundry for non-Christians to see.

Does Paul, especially in verse 6, seem to be more disturbed by the fact that Christians cannot settle their disagreements with one another, or by the fact that this is happening in front of non-Christians?

_____

_____

7. What does Paul mean by the first sentence of verse 7? How have Christians been defeated?

_____

_____

8. Would Paul be happier for the Christians if they set up a Christian court in their congregation? Or is Paul saying that two Christians should be able to settle their differences in love, and that the need to call in a third party (no matter who) to judge such a dispute means that both parties involved are somehow selfish, and therefore acting in a non-Christian way?

_____

_____

9. Compare verse 7 to Matthew 5:39-42. Are these passages saying the same thing or does one provide an illustration for the other?

10. What would Paul have to say about the attitude of members of your congregation toward taking each other to court?

11. What problems does your congregation have that are similar to those experienced by the Corinthian church?

12. What kind of image does your congregation's method of dealing with problems present to those outside the congregation?

13. In these verses Paul simply says that Christians have no need to go to secular courts to solve their problems. In saying this, he does not imply that the Roman or Corinthian courts are unjust. In other words, whether or not the courts were capable of solving the problem of Christians is not the point. Paul is concerned that they

deal with the problems amongst themselves.

Even if Christians consider today's courts to be fair, should they take their disputes to court? Why or why not?

---

14. Review verses 1-8 once again and observe how Paul sets the church against the rest of the world. Would he still find these two groups so clearly defined in our "Christian" country today? Does the answer to this question have any bearing on the discussion about lawsuits?

---

15. Note the location in this letter of Paul's discussion of lawsuits. The sections before and after it both deal with sexual immorality. Does this give us a hint as to what was involved in these lawsuit(s) among the Corinthians?

Inheriting the kingdom of God: 6:9-11

In verse 9 Paul changes his way of talking about the Christians. Instead of church against world, he now speaks of the "wicked" against the "kingdom of God." He then presents a list of those apparently included in the class of the wicked, and concludes with a comment on the changed nature of the Corinthian Christians.

1. In verse 9 Paul speaks of inheriting the kingdom of

God. The kingdom of God is a theme that was central to Jesus' preaching (e.g., Matt. 4:23; Luke 4:43). Jesus sometimes spoke of the kingdom of God as already present, and sometimes as something yet to come (in the future). What do you understand Paul to mean when he speaks of inheriting this kingdom of God?

_____

_____

2. Compare the list of persons in verses 9b-10 with the sins mentioned in Galatians 5:19-21. Why does Paul choose to include these particular groups of people in this Corinthian list?

        1 Cor. 6:9b-10   Gal. 5:19-21

3. What do verses 9-10, together with verse 11, tell us about the Corinthian congregation?

4. Look at the acts in verse 11: "washed," "sanctified," and "justified." Paul mentions these actions after speaking about the kingdom of God. How do these words fit in with the kingdom of God? Do you see any meaning in their order?

Bodies for the Lord and not for immorality: 6:12-20
In this section, Paul picks up his discussion of sexuality, going from immorality (chap. 5) to a Christian view of the body (6:12-20).

Paul starts off in verse 12 by arguing with a quote, the source of which he does not give. Behind the Corinthian ideas may have been a kind of thinking called Gnosticism. This, as described in Session 2, was a belief held by some people in those days that only knowledge *gnosis* was important, and that the body came second. This led some Gnostics to say that what people did with their bodies did not matter. Gnosticism threatened first-century Christianity and influenced it at many points. While Gnosticism is clearly in the background of 1 Corinthians 6:12-20, we are not sure that it can be used to interpret this passage.

Paul begins with two sayings that must have been popular among the Corinthians: "Everything is permissible for me" and "Food for the stomach and the stomach for food." These slogans may have been Gnostic sayings that the Corinthian Christians also endorsed. On the other hand, they may have been statements that Paul himself made earlier regarding Jewish food laws. In either case, Paul begins by making clear what such statements should mean for Christians.

1. Notice that Paul does not reverse the statement "everything is permissible for me." Rather, he contrasts "permissible" with "not . . . beneficial" and being "mastered." What does Paul mean by verse 12?

_____

_____

2. From verses 13 to 20, Paul uses each verse to make one specific point about the body. Jot down the main point about the body from each verse.

Verse 13 _____

Verse 14 _____

Verse 16 _____

Verse 17 _____

Verse 18 _____

Verse 19 _____

Verse 20 _____

3. Compare what Paul says in verse 13 about eating and about food to what Jesus says in Mark 7:19, and to Paul's discussion about food sacrificed to idols in 1 Corinthians 8 (especially v. 8). How are these three passages alike? How are they different?

4. Notice that Paul does not disagree with the proposition "Food for the stomach and the stomach for food," saying rather that God will destroy them both. Consider this further by reading 1 Corinthians 15:35-50, where Paul argues for the resurrection of the body. How do these two passages fit together?

5. Why does Paul, in his discussion about sexual immorality, bring in these thoughts on food and the stomach? No doubt the Corinthians had made a connection between the two: (a) since the stomach (as a part of the body) is only temporary, we can satisfy our physical desires for food by totally setting aside all food laws and restrictions; and (b) if this is true for the stomach and for food, then it must also be true for the body and for sexual desires: since the body is only temporary, we can satisfy our physical sexual desires by setting aside all commandments against sexual immorality and adultery.

Paul says that though the first argument may hold true (food laws may be disregarded, since both the food and the stomach will be dissolved by God at death), the second one does not follow from it. Hence, "the body is not meant for sexual immorality, but for the Lord" (v. 13b).

Verses 14-20 go on to argue that sexual intercourse differs from eating food because of the meaning it has for the person. Follow through the rest of these verses and outline Paul's line of reasoning.

6. Paul, in verse 18, claims that when it comes to a person's body, sexual sins differ from all other sins. They not only wrong another person, but they also harm the person doing the act. Can you think of other acts which would be like sins against one's own body? Or what does Paul mean by "all other [than sexual] sins a man commits are outside his body"?

7. List the things that Paul says about our bodies in verses 19 and 20.

8. Verse 19 gives us a definition of the body: it is a temple of the Holy Spirit. Compare this verse with 1 Corinthians 3:16-17. How are these two passages the same and/or where do they say different things?

9. After having worked through verses 12-20, what did you learn about how Christians ought to use their bodies?

_____

_____

_____

Summary
In this lesson we have seen that Paul discourages Christians from taking each other to court. Paul shows that it is bad enough to have disagreement, but to take such problems outside of Christian circles to pagan judges is even worse. Paul suggests that the Corinthians should rather suffer some loss than to go to court. Having scolded the Corinthians for not being able to settle their disputes without going to non-Christian judges, Paul returns to his former theme to also criticize them for their attitude toward their bodies and sexuality. Paul reminds the Corinthians that their bodies are temples of the Holy Spirit and, as such, should be treated with reverence.

From the matter of sexuality in chapter 6, Paul is reminded that the Corinthians asked him some questions about marriage, and he goes on to answer them in the next chapter.

Session 8. Marry since there is so much immorality

1 Corinthians 7:1-24

So far, chapters 1—6 have shown that Paul wrote the Corinthian letter to deal with issues that came to his attention through sources such as Chloe's people. (See 1 Cor. 1:11.) Beginning with chapter 7, Paul answers the problems raised by the Corinthian Christians in a letter which they wrote to Paul.

This chapter deals with a number of questions, all related to the theme of marriage. Paul's discussion can be divided into two general areas: (a) concerning the unmarried (whether they are to marry); and (b) concerning the married (whether they should continue living together).

Paul's thoughts on marriage, as presented in this chapter, are easily misunderstood. Very often Paul has been criticized—sometimes fairly, sometimes unfairly—for having a low view of marriage. In working through this chapter, however, a number of things need to be kept in mind, so as to give Paul a fair reading.

First of all, we need to look at Paul's intention in writing chapter 7. Paul is *not* making an effort to sort out all his thoughts on the subject of marriage. Rather, he is answering specific questions asked by the people of Corinth. So, to understand Paul's answer, it would be most helpful to know just what the questions were. Unfortunately, however, we cannot be sure what the questions were. Thus, the best we can do is to approach Paul's answers with openness.

Secondly, we need to remember that the Corinthians' questions reflect a specific controversy in their congregation. Some of the people within the church (probably those with Jewish background) thought of marriage as essential. Other people (possibly those influenced by certain Greek ideas) regarded marriage as inferior to celibacy (voluntary singleness). Still others believed that upon becoming a Christian, all existing social relationships, including marriage, had no more meaning or were no longer binding.

So Paul is not writing about marriage in a vacuum. Rather, he is speaking to specific situations in which specific ideas already existed.

Better to marry than to burn with passion: 7:1-9

During the days of the early church, many Christians were inclined to think of celibacy as more desirable than marriage. Some of the people in the Corinthian church also shared this view. In verses 1-7 Paul speaks about this attitude. At least two questions seem to underlie his discussion: (a) Is it permissible for Christians to marry? (b) Are married couples to continue normal sexual relations after becoming Christians? In replying to these questions, Paul sets out basic principles on which the remainder of the chapter builds.

1. How did Paul come to know that the Corinthian church had problems concerning marriage (v. 1)?

___

2. What might have been the Corinthians' questions which caused Paul to respond the way he does in verses 1 and 2?

Question A: ___

Question B: _____

To understand verse 1b, we need to know that neither the Jewish nor the Greek culture made any case for celibacy (voluntary singleness). Both groups had a high view of marriage. Paul may not be saying that celibacy is so much better than marriage, but only that it is not wrong to live a celibate life.

Verse 2 explains the meaning of verse 1. Paul says that some conditions in life make marriage necessary. Though it is all right not to marry (v. 1b), the general rule is that "each man should have his own wife" and "each woman [should have] her own husband" for the sake of morality. Paul does not say that marriage serves no purpose beyond that of acting as a guard against immorality, but it does serve that purpose.

3. How much emphasis do you—as an individual and as a congregation—place on marriage? For what reasons?

_____
_____
_____

4. What is your attitude toward remaining single? Why?

_____
_____
_____

5. What advice does Paul give to the husband and to the wife in verses 3-4?

Verse 3: _____

_____

Verse 4: _____

6. What can we gather about Paul's thoughts of equality of the sexes from these verses?

_____

_____

7. In verse 5 Paul discusses sexual intercourse as the privilege of each partner in a marriage. This privilege is not to be denied each other except in specific cases. Paul lays down four limitations of this general rule. A married couple could interrupt normal sexual practices: (a) by mutual agreement; (b) for a time; (c) for the purpose of prayer; and (d) with the intention of coming together again.

When Paul uses the phrase "do not deprive each other" it suggests that some people in Corinth were doing exactly what he says they are not to do. Some of the Corinthians had come to the conclusion that sexual intercourse was sinful and, as Christians, they had to abstain from it.

What do you see as the proper attitude toward sexual relations between husband and wife?

_____

_____

In verse 5 Paul speaks of married partners separating temporarily in order to devote themselves to prayer. Why would Paul say this?

Judaic law (some of the Corinthians were of Jewish background) held that a newlywed man was to be excused from some prayer because his marital situation meant that he was otherwise preoccupied. But, Paul says, in spite of the fact that marriage and sexual relations may take away (temporarily) from prayer, this does not mean that sexual relations in marriage are evil. Paul grants that it is all right to abstain, by mutual consent, from full marital relations for the purpose of prayer, but only for a time, after which the physical part of the marriage should resume again.

8. The major problem in trying to understand verse 6 is in deciding what exactly it refers to: to what is Paul making a "concession"? At least three possibilities must be taken into account: (1) the concession refers to verse 2: Paul is not commanding marriage, but merely conceding that it may be entered into; (2) the concession refers to verse 5b: Paul is not commanding married partners to reunite after separating for prayer, he is merely conceding that they may; (3) the concession refers to all of verse 5: Paul is not commanding married couples to deprive each other, but is simply conceding (to the Corinthians promoting self-denial) that if the reason is prayer, it is possible to separate temporarily.

Which of these three options do you consider to best interpret what Paul is trying to say in verse 6?

_____

_____

_____

9. To what do the "gifts" of verse 7 refer?

_____

_____

Verses 7 and 8 raise the question of Paul's past. Look at these verses for a moment and consider whether Paul was single, married, widowed, or divorced. Verse 8 tells us that Paul was unmarried at the time of writing 1 Corinthians. Anything beyond that fact, however, is more complicated. The main reason to believe that Paul had never been married is that he never explicitly refers to or even alludes to his (former) wife. The New Testament nowhere mentions any wife or children of Paul.

On the other hand, several reasons suggest that, at one point, he was married. One reason is based simply on his understanding of married life. A stronger reason to support this case comes out of the first-century Jewish law: rabbis, in order to be allowed to sit in judgment in a capital offense, needed to be married and have children. Paul, who was a Jewish rabbi, and did sit in judgment of a capital offense (Acts 26:10), must have fulfilled these Jewish requirements and therefore had been married at some point.

10. Verses 8 and 9 form transition verses. In what way do they sum up the previous section, verses 1-7?

_____

_____

_____

God has called us to live in peace: 7:10-24
Verses 8-9 have reinforced that which Paul has said earlier: the most fortunate state is that of the unmarried person who is under no pressure to marry. This then raises the question: What about those who are married? In verses 10-24 Paul addresses himself to this question.

The next unit of material (vv. 10-24) falls naturally into three segments:

(a) Verses 10-11, dealing with marriages in which both husband and wife are believers;

(b) Verses 12-16, dealing with mixed marriages, where the one partner is a Christian and the other is not; and

(c) Verses 17-24, giving the principle underlying Paul's advice.

A. When facing separation or divorce: 7:10-11
1. Whom is Paul addressing in verses 10 and 11?

2. What advice does Paul give regarding marriage?

(a) to the wife: _____

(b) to the husband: _____

3. According to verse 10, the prohibition of separation and divorce between Christians seems absolute. But in verse 11 Paul includes a statement that shows his awareness that marriages can and do break up. What two alternatives does he give regarding separation?

(a) _____

(b) _____

4. In verse 10 Paul says that the advice he is giving to the married is not his own but that which was passed on by Jesus. The Gospels record numerous sayings of Jesus concerning marriage. Look up the following passages and write down their advice concerning marriage.

(a) Matthew 5:27-32 _____

(b) Matthew 19:3-12 _____

(c) Mark 10:2-12 _____

(d) Luke 16:18 _____

5. Jesus' teachings on marriage, and especially on divorce, have given Christians many difficulties. Various Christian churches have much diversity of opinion as to Jesus' meaning in his sayings about divorce. Some churches disallow all divorce; others allow it in the case of infidelity, but then refuse to marry either of the spouses; yet others allow divorce and will remarry the "innocent" spouse; and still others are willing to allow the remarriage of either spouse, providing the person is repentant and genuinely wants to begin married life on a better foundation of Christian values.

What stand do you think the church ought to take in this regard?

_____

_____

6. What is the role of the church in a situation where two Christians do separate?

_____

_____

7. What is the role of the church in a situation where a Christian wants to get married, and where one of the persons is separated or divorced?

_____

_____

B. Believers caught in mixed marriages: 7:12-16
Two kinds of mixed marriages are considered in verses

12-16. In verses 12-14 Paul discusses the situation of an unbeliever willing to continue a marriage with a believer, while in verses 15-16 he turns his attention to an unbeliever refusing to continue living with a Christian spouse.

1. Who are the "rest" that Paul is addressing in verse 12?

___

___

Notice that in verse 12 Paul claims to be speaking on his *own* authority. This does not mean that he expects his words to be taken less seriously but only that in this situation he cannot offer the support of any words of Jesus—who had probably never been faced by a case of a mixed marriage.

2. What advice does Paul set out, in these verses, for the Christian married to a non-Christian?

(a) advice to the husband: ___

___

(b) advice to the wife: ___

___

3. What reasons does Paul give for appealing to believing husbands or wives to remain married to their unbelieving partners (v. 14)?

___

___

___

4. Paul thinks it important for a Christian to stay in a marriage where the spouse is a non-Christian. What strengths or weaknesses would this kind of a marriage have?

___

5. What advice does Paul give in the case of the unbelieving partner wanting to separate from a believing spouse?

6. What reason does Paul give in verse 15 for advising separation in certain situations?

7. Reread verses 14 and 16. Are they saying the same thing or something contradictory?

8. There are four possibilities of Christian and non-Christian marriages:

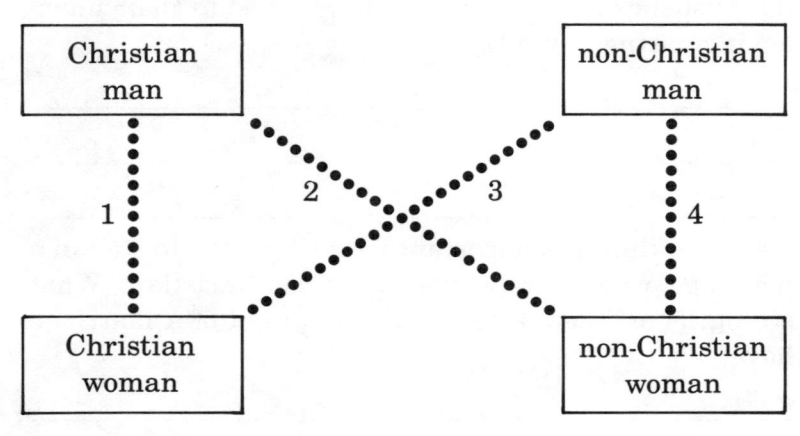

```
┌─────────────┐                    ┌─────────────┐
│  Christian  │        2      3    │ non-Christian│
│     man     │╲         ╱         │     man     │
└─────────────┘ ╲       ╱          └─────────────┘
      │          ╲     ╱                  │
    1 │           ╲   ╱                 4 │
      │            ╲ ╱                    │
      │            ╱ ╲                    │
      │           ╱   ╲                   │
┌─────────────┐  ╱     ╲          ┌─────────────┐
│  Christian  │ ╱       ╲         │ non-Christian│
│    woman    │╱         ╲        │    woman    │
└─────────────┘                    └─────────────┘
```

Does Paul seem to give a preference to any of these combinations over any others?

9. What difference would there be between a situation in which a Christian marries a non-Christian and a situation in which one non-Christian who marries another non-Christian later becomes a believer?

10. Sum up Paul's overall advice regarding marriage and separation in these verses (10-16).

C. Retain the place in life assigned you: 7:17-24

Verses 17-24 give the underlying principle of Paul's advice on marriage. The central theme which Paul has until now presupposed and which he now develops is outlined in verse 17 and verse 24. These two verses, which provide a frame for this section (v. 17 at the beginning and v. 24 at the end), outline this principle: Christians are to remain in the situation in which they are or to which God has called them. Later Paul explains why he says this (vv. 26, 29-31), but we will look now at how Paul lays out the theme of "remain as you are."

Even though verses 17-24 refer primarily to circumcision and slavery, they are closely related to the overall discussion of marriage.

1. What is the main point of verse 17?

2. To which two examples does Paul apply this rule?

3. What do verses 18-23 tell us about the type of people in the Corinthian congregation?

4. What advice does Paul give to the circumcised and to the uncircumcised in verse 18?

Circumcision was the Jewish ritual which distinguished Jews from other people. Jewish boys were normally circumcised when they were eight days old. A man converted to Judaism also received circumcision.

5. What do verses 18-19 imply about the presence or absence of circumcision?

6. Verse 19 must have seemed like nonsense to Paul's Jewish readers. On the one hand, Paul says that circumcision is nothing; on the other hand, he says that God's

commandments are to be kept. For a (Christian) Jew, Paul's argument would have seemed totally illogical: to keep God's commandment meant to be circumcised (Gen. 17:10-14).

What does Paul mean in verse 19? See also Romans 2:25-29.

_____

_____

_____

7. In verse 20 Paul says that "Each one should remain in the situation which he was in when God called him." What kind of things would be included, and what kind of things would not be included, in this "situation" that Paul mentions?

_____

_____

_____

8. Is Paul saying the same thing or two different things in verses 20 and 21?

_____

_____

_____

Verses 17-20 show that all outward circumstances of life are relatively unimportant. But Paul also says (v. 21) that he does not believe that a person *has to* remain in the state in which they were before they became a Christian. The calling of God is as important as the situation in which the person is called. Christians are not to remain stagnant within a set position in life as much as they are to remain faithful to God's calling within that situation.

9. Why is social status as a free person or a slave unimportant for a Christian?

10. Can you think of any circumstances in which these verses on slavery have been used out of context, to keep some people in positions of power over others?

11. What does Paul mean in verse 23? What does it mean to be "slaves of men"?

Summary
So far Paul has discussed the different possible relationships between a man and woman. He has addressed relationships in marriage, then given some advice to those presently not married (including the widowed), and has gone on from there to some specific situations in marriage. After a tangent to explain his reasons for some of his thoughts, he now turns his attention to the unmarried (v. 25).

Session 9. Virgins devoted to the Lord in both body and spirit

1 Corinthians 7:25-40

Paul addresses his new subject by "Now about virgins." Who the virgins were is unclear; it will be discussed in the comments on verses 35-40 below. Read verse 25 and note that once again Paul is careful to define the nature of his advice. He states quite clearly that he has "no commandment from the Lord" but that his judgment is trustworthy.

In verse 26 Paul declares that "I think that it is good for you to remain as you are." This is a theme which he has already been developing throughout chapter 7. But in verse 26 Paul adds the main reason that his advice has taken this turn: it is "because of the present crisis."

What exactly is this "present crisis"? Some interpreters suggest that this must be a reference to some unusually difficult situations through which the Corinthians were passing at the time. It seems far more likely, however, that Paul is referring to the crisis which he explains further in verses 29-31. For Paul, "the time is short" (v. 29), the world "is passing away" (v. 31). This will be examined more closely in verses 29-31 below.

1. What is Paul's advice to both the married and the unmarried in verses 26 and 27?

_____

_____

2. In verse 28 Paul says that "those who marry will face many troubles in this life."
(a) What kind of troubles is Paul speaking of here?

(b) What might this tell us about Paul's own life?

(c) Are there times today when people should be advised not to get married? If so, give an example.

3. In verse 29 we find the phrase "the time is short." This is probably a reference to the return of Christ (which Paul may have expected in his lifetime). This reference helps us to understand the advice that Paul is giving in this entire chapter: since the end is near, don't bother changing your state in life (getting married, for example).

Note that in verses 29-31 there are five "as if" phrases. List these.

These repeated "as if" phrases emphasize that the Christian should as much as possible live in this age as though the coming age were already here. The values of the age to come are the ones that will last.

So when Paul says that "those who have wives should live as if they had none," he does not mean that they should live a celibate life within the framework of marriage (because he has already advised against this earlier). Rather, married persons must recognize that the institution in which they are involved will pass away.

4. What do we do with verses 29-31 today? How do Paul's words apply to us?

___

___

5. In verse 32 Paul continues his thoughts from verse 28. Marriage will bring with it many "troubles in this life" (v. 28), and Paul would have the Corinthians be "free from [these kinds of] concern."

How might, according to verses 32-35, and according to your experience, an unmarried person be better able to "please the Lord" than a married person?

___

___

6. How does verse 35 sum up Paul's thoughts to this point?

___

___

Verses 36-38 are hard to understand. The main problem involves the words "the virgin he is engaged to." In the Greek, the words mean simply "his virgin." Who is the virgin and who is meant by "he" (the person to whom the virgin "belongs")? Several suggestions can be offered:

(a) The simplest choice is that the man and the woman he is engaged to ("his virgin") are uncertain as to whether or not they should actually get married, thinking it may not be the correct Christian thing to do. (The NIV translates the verse as if this is the best meaning: "the virgin he is engaged to.") If Paul is addressing this kind of a couple, then he is telling them to go ahead and get married—there's nothing wrong with that.

(b) A second possibility for understanding this section is that "his virgin" can mean "his daughter." In this case, the man to whom the virgin "belongs" is the father, who according to the custom of the day was responsible for his daughter's marriage. If Paul is speaking to this situation, then he is saying go ahead and marry (your daughter to some man)—there's nothing wrong with that.

(c) A third alternative is that the man and the woman ("his virgin") are living together but not having any physical relations. Paul, in realizing that this kind of a "spiritual" marriage may be quite a strain on both parties and is, therefore, better consummated into a full marriage, says there's nothing wrong with such an "ordinary" marriage.

7. Trace these three possibilities through verses 36-38, noticing how each sentence would fit into each of the possible meanings.

8. Which of these three possibilities do you think best fits verses 36-38?

9. Verses 39-40 add one final thought on an issue related to marriage: are widows to remarry? What is Paul's answer to this question, and in what two ways does he qualify it?

In verses 39 and 40 Paul is saying something specific to Christians wondering about the need to follow the Jewish laws: he is saying yes, a man and a woman who are married belong to each other until one of them dies. But no, the woman is not required to marry inside her dead husband's family. (See Deut. 25:5-10.) She is free to marry anyone she wishes (as long as he is a Christian).

10. What is Paul's advice to the widow in verse 40?

11. Why does Paul add "and I think that I too have the Spirit of God" in verse 40?

12. How do you apply what Paul says in chapter 7 about singleness, marriage, separation, and divorce to today's situation in your church?

Summary

In chapter 7 Paul has begun to answer some of the questions which the Corinthians had asked him. The first question he discusses is on marriage, concerning not only the married but also the unmarried. He explains his views on different situations in marriage, and also speaks about celibacy, singleness, and remarriage.

In the midst of his discussion on marriage-related matters, Paul also drops some other pointers. Most notable of these is his theme of "stay in the situation in which God has called you."

The Corinthian letter, following chapter 7, goes on to discuss a number of issues about which the Corinthians had also requested some answers from Paul.